Quit for Life

A Clinical Guide to Smoking Cessation

Kathryn T. Vullo, Ph.D.

Ronald P. Vullo, Ph.D.

ISBN: 1-4140-0879-1 (e-book)
ISBN: 1-4140-0878-3 (Paperback)

This book is printed on acid free paper.

In Memory of John and Frances Klein

Introduction

- The Dangers of Smoking

- Reasons for Quitting

- Why You've Failed Before

- How Is This Program Different?

- How This Program Works

- How Long Will This Take?

Congratulations! You have taken the first step toward giving up cigarettes permanently. The program you are about to undertake is a comprehensive intervention aimed at helping you to quit permanently. Written by two doctors: an educational specialist and a clinical psychologist with specialization in behavioral medicine, this program is based on the most recent research proven to be effective in aiding people to change their lifestyles. It was created from many years of experience providing successful multifaceted smoking cessation programs to individuals and groups.

You will find this program to be strongly educational. We know that this is the key to success in life. By understanding your lifestyle, the choices you make, your strengths and weaknesses, you will be able to implement the interventions in a manner that is most fitting to you. How many times have you tried to quit with a method that treats all smokers alike? While you may have found some of the methods to be applicable to your situation, you may have felt that you weren't benefiting fully from the program.

You will be provided with education and options regarding smoking cessation. From the information presented, you will be able to make informed decisions about the best way for you to quit, and to cope with the many challenges that face you. This will increase not only your success in quitting, but your long-term success at remaining a nonsmoker.

Because this program is based on real clinical research, you will find references to that research throughout the book. These citations should give you confidence, knowing that many scientists have been working on this research for many years.

The Dangers of Smoking

According to the American Cancer Society (2002;1996):

- Tobacco smoke contains over 4,000 chemical compounds including at least 43 carcinogenic (cancer causing) substances.

- Smoking decreases a person's life expectancy by an average of 7 years.

- Smokers are ten times more likely than nonsmokers to develop lung cancer.

- Smoking is responsible for 87% of lung cancer.

- Tobacco use accounts for 30% of all cancer deaths in the United States.

- Cancer of the mouth, esophagus, larynx, kidney, bladder, pancreas, and the cervix have smoking as a common cause.

- Chronic Bronchitis is a common health problem for smokers.

- Smoking is the major cause of emphysema.

- Almost 180,000 Americans die each year from cardiovascular disease caused by smoking.

- Cigarette smoking is responsible for 65,000 deaths due to Chronic Obstructive Pulmonary Disease (COPD), which includes bronchitis and emphysema.

- Children of smokers have a greater chance of developing colds, bronchitis, pneumonia, chronic coughs, ear infections and reduced lung function.

- Pregnant women who smoke endanger the health and lives of their unborn babies.

Reasons for Quitting

According to the U.S. Surgeon General (September, 1990), the following are benefits of smoking cessation:

- People who quit smoking, regardless of age, live longer than those who continue to smoke.

- Smokers who quit before the age of 50 have half the risk of dying in the next 15 years compared with those who continue to smoke.

- Quitting smoking reduces the risk of coronary heart disease and cardiovascular disease.

- Smoking cessation substantially decreases the risk of lung, oral, esophageal, laryngeal, pancreatic, bladder and cervical cancers.

- Stopping smoking will reduce the effects of secondary smoke on your family. Nonsmokers married to heavy smokers (1 or more packs per day) have 2 to 3 times the risk of lung cancer compared with those married to nonsmokers.

It is never to late to quit smoking, According to a report in the American Journal of Public Health (2002), people can live a lot longer, regardless of the age at which they quit smoking. While younger people benefit the most, even smokers over the age of 65 can extend their life by quitting. Male smokers who quit at age 35 added between 6.9 years and 8.5 years to their lives when compared with those who continued to smoke. Thirty-five year old women could expect to live between 6.1 and 7.7 years longer than if they continued smoking. A sixty-five year old male could expect to add 1.4 to 2 year to his life, while a 65 year old female could live 2.7 to 3.7 years longer (CA Cancer Journal for Clinicians, 2002).

Now that you can anticipate living longer, you can contemplate how to spend all of the money you will save over a lifetime from quitting. For a smoker who smokes a pack a day, you can expect to save approximately $1,600.00 each year by quitting; $3,200.00 per year for those who smoke two packs per day. Over thirty years, that adds up to $48,000 (or $96,000 for a two-pack-a-day habit). That doesn't include the thousands of dollars saved in lost wages from sick days or medical expenses for smoke-related illnesses. You can calculate the savings from breaking your smoking habit at the Arizona Smoker's Helpline at: http://ashline/ASH/quit

You've probably heard these statistics over and over. You have your own personal reasons for kicking the smoking habit, whether it is the negative impact that it has on your family, poor modeling for your children, chronic bronchitis, diabetes, or other health problems. Or maybe you are just plain sick and tired of feeling controlled by a negative habit. This program will help you identify your reasons for smoking, and assist you in making appropriate changes in your lifestyle to permanently stop smoking.

Why You've Failed Before

Each year nearly 10 million people try to quit for at least one day during the American Cancer Society's Great American Smokeout. Of these, approximately three hundred thousand remain nonsmokers after 5 days (American Cancer Society, 2002). That's a five-day success rate of only 3%.

On average, for smokers who have quit cold turkey less than 10% will have long term success (American Lung Association, 2003). Chances are, you have made many attempts to quit smoking before. You may have been successful for a week, a month, or even a year, but for some reason, you became re-addicted. Smoking cessation is not easy. If it were, we would all be nonsmokers.

There are as many ways to stop smoking as there are reasons for wanting to quit. Unfortunately, not all are successful. Most smoking cessation programs address either the physical addiction *or* the emotional dependency on cigarettes. Research shows that the pharmacological and behavioral processes that result in tobacco addiction are similar to those that determine addiction to drugs such as cocaine and heroin. Therefore, to be successful you must focus on *both* the physiological and behavioral components of addiction.

Breaking the habit is difficult. Not returning to the habit can be just as challenging. If you've been successful in quitting before, something happened that led you to slip back into the habit. Face it, if you didn't, you wouldn't be reading this. If you're like most smokers, you are probably smoking more now than before you initially quit. If not, consider yourself lucky. An effective smoking program should address relapse prevention (methods of increasing your likelihood of remaining a nonsmoker). This program spends as much time teaching you how to maintain your success as it does teaching you how to effectively quit. The act of quitting takes only a day, but avoiding the temptations ahead of you will remain an active part of your life for a long time.

How is this Program Different?

As you know from past attempts to stop smoking, lighting a cigarette is not the only behavior that needs to change. In addition to breaking the physical addiction to nicotine, you must change many factors including social factors, coping skills, self-confidence, and social support, while substituting alternative behaviors to successfully break the smoking habit. This program addresses the physical and emotional addiction processes, as well as social factors while teaching you to use new coping strategies, relaxation, and relapse prevention.

Most smoking cessation programs focus on either breaking the physical addiction or breaking the emotional dependency on cigarettes. If a program is comprehensive enough to address both of these vital issues, they often fail in providing the support needed during this difficult time, as well as teaching substitute methods of coping with stress. The Quit for Life program is designed to address all of these issues, as well as to educate you about yourself and your choices of behavior. It will enable you to gain control over your behavior, and your health. It will allow you to identify your strengths and use them to make permanent changes. Hopefully you will use these skills to help you succeed in other aspects of your life.

How This Program Works

This program is designed to take you through the quitting process step by step. While we set the pace, week by week, you are free to set your own schedule within the weeks. For example, if it's easiest for you to set aside Monday evenings, then that's when you should focus on the program. You should set aside a specific time each week to read and complete the assignments. This shouldn't require more than 20-30 minutes each week. You owe it to yourself to dedicate your full attention for a brief period of time to each chapter, and not read it intermittently like a novel.

In addition to the topics briefly discussed so far, other topics include:

- Reasons for quitting

- Should I wean off cigarettes, or go "Cold Turkey?"

- The patch, or not the patch - that is the question!

- Hypnosis: does it really work?

- Avoiding weight gain

- Cravings

- Self-rewards for a job well done

- Coping with stress

- Self-talk

- Substituting other pleasurable activities

- How to remain a nonsmoker

How Long Will This Take?

You can expect to be cigarette free by the first day of week four at the latest!   While this may not be as quick as you would like, the pace is established in a way that maximizes long-term success. Just as a marathon runner would not be successful by sprinting through the entire race, following the appropriate pace leads to success. If you choose to quit "cold turkey," or with the aid of nicotine gum or patch, you can expect to quit sooner. The program will help you to select the most appropriate method and time frame for you. These choices will help you select the methods that are most comfortable for you and allow you to maximize your own personal strengths.

The program consists of six weekly units. Each week you will learn about your own patterns and habits while increasing your insight into your own personal lifestyle. While all smokers have many things in common, each have their own personality styles and their own reasons for smoking and quitting.

The weekly objectives of the program are:

Week 1: Increased Self-Awareness

1. Identifying Your Reasons for Quitting

2. Increasing Your Awareness of Your Smoking Patterns

3. Self-Monitoring

4. Weaning Down vs. "Cold Turkey"

5. The Patch or Not the Patch: That is the Question…

6. Bupropion: Wellbutrin, Zyban

Week 2: Begin Now

    1. Review of Self-Monitoring Sheets

    2. Fears of Quitting

    3. Rewards

    4. Begin Now!

Week 3: Coping with Stress

    1. Examining Your Progress

    2. Reduce by Another One-third

    3. Breaking Old Habits

    4. STRESSED is More Than DESSERTS Spelled Backwards

    5. Assessing your Current Coping Skills

    6. Increasing your Coping Skills

    7. Deep Breathing and Deep Muscle Relaxation Training

    8. Stop Smoking Contract

    9. Reward Yourself

Week 4: Quit Today

    1. Reviewing Your Progress

    2. Hypnosis

    3. Quit Today!

    4. Understanding How Your Body is Already Repairing Itself:

        Withdrawal Effects

    5. Fighting Cravings and Urges

    6. Identifying Alternative Pleasurable Activities

    7. Avoiding Weight Gain

Week 5: Relapse Prevention

1. Relapse Prevention: Remaining a Nonsmoker

2. Identifying High Risk Situations

3. Setbacks and Slips

4. Combating Rationalizations

5. Reward Yourself

Week 6: Remaining a Nonsmoker for Life

1. Reviewing Your Success

2. Assessing New Coping Skills

3. Anticipating High Risk Situations

4. Remaining a Nonsmoker for Life!

This program has been designed from the most recent clinical research, as well as many years of experience providing successful multifaceted behavioral programs to individuals and groups. We are certain that if you follow the weekly program and dedicate yourself fully to eliminating your smoking, you will succeed in both quitting, and staying smoke free. If however, during the course of the program, you have a setback, you should go back to where you were last successful and continue the program.

We recognize that occasional stressors or crises do evolve unexpectedly while one is trying to break unhealthy habits. We tend to turn to these habits as a primary means of coping, leading to a "setback" or "relapse." DO NOT allow this opportunity to become an excuse to give up the progress that you made. Each additional setback sabotages your confidence and self-efficacy, and makes it more difficult for you to succeed.

If you are not 100% convinced that you want to be smoke free in the next month, or you have in the back of your mind that you can "cheat" and have one cigarette, or skip certain sections of the program, you may wish to reevaluate whether you are ready to make this important lifestyle change at this time. This program will work for any smoker, from social smokers to hard core, four pack a day smokers, but *only if you are completely motivated* to dedicate yourself to changing your lifestyle.

You can begin on Week One as soon as you are ready!

Week One: Increasing Your Awareness

- Identifying Your Reasons for Quitting

- Increasing Your Awareness of Your Smoking Patterns

- Self-Monitoring

- Weaning Down vs. "Cold Turkey"

- The Patch or Not the Patch: That is the Question...

- Bupropion: Wellbutrin, Zyban

Welcome to week one of Quit for Life! Congratulations on your decision to improve your life. Week one is designed to increase your self-awareness so that you can prepare for the major lifestyle change you have chosen. Let's get started!

Identifying Your Reasons for Quitting

At this time, you have made an important decision and a commitment to stop smoking. This is a difficult undertaking, with numerous benefits resulting from your success. The introductory chapter outlined twelve dangers associated with smoking. There are hundreds of dangers associated with tar and nicotine. On a positive note, each of the dangers imply a benefit for quitting. Just as people begin smoking and continue smoking for different reasons, they quit for different reasons.

You have many personal reasons for quitting smoking at this time. It is important to be aware of these reasons because they are the source of your motivation. Whether you are quitting for health reasons, because of the effect on your children, or you feel that you are being controlled by your habit, you have made the important decision to stop smoking. Below, list as many reasons as you can for stopping smoking. Be sure to list only those that pertain to you specifically (for example: While "increased risk for prostate cancer" may be a legitimate reason for some, it is not a significant motivator if you are a middle aged woman).

My Reasons For Quitting:

_____

_____

_____

_____

_____

_____

_____

_____

_____

Review your list to make sure that you didn't leave any out. Make sure that you include a reason for each of the following categories:

- health factors/life expectancy
- social factors
- impact on others, and
- expense (calculate per year).

Common reasons for quitting include: risk for cardiovascular diseases, respiratory disease, or cancer; negative impact on your partner, poor modeling for your children, risk of birth defects in pregnant women, the cost of an expensive habit, and feeling socially ostracized at work or social gatherings that do not allow smoking.

Now go through the list once again and prioritize your reasons. Assign the number "1" for the most important reason. Then, assign number "2" for the second most important reason, and so on.

Keep this list and review it periodically. This will be extremely important in the next few weeks when you feel cravings and urges to smoke. These will act as cues, or reminders, that allow you to focus on your reasons for quitting and will be helpful in realistically challenging your rationalizations that will tempt you to return to smoking.

Increasing Your Awareness of Your Smoking Patterns

Smoking is a learned behavior. The first cigarette you ever had was likely a strange, uncomfortable situation. With practice and observation, you learned how to smoke without coughing, or how to exhale smoke through your nose without blowing out unmentionable bodily mucous. You've learned how to use cigarettes as a stress management technique. You've learned that having a cigarette in your mouth when you are angry allows for a more fluid expulsion of four-letter expletives. *Being a nonsmoker now needs to be learned.*

Think about that Psychology 101 course you took in college... (No, not the nonsense that suggests that smokers are orally fixated because they were weaned prematurely from their mother's breast, or that cigarettes are nothing more than phallic symbols.) We are referring to the behaviorists, namely B. F. Skinner and Pavlov. A quick refresher: Operant conditioning (a la Skinner) demonstrates that behaviors that result in pleasure or reinforcement are likely to reoccur. Smoking has brought you many years of pleasure. For instance, you felt that smoking benefited you by helping you to deal with stress. Because of its positive effect of lowering your perceived level of stress, it became reinforced as a coping tool. Hence, the behavior of smoking is likely to reoccur. Skinner also demonstrated that behaviors were learned and became reinforced when they allowed the individual to successfully avoided negative consequences. How many times have you smoked a cigarette simply to avoid feelings of nicotine withdrawal? Like Skinner's rats who learned to push a lever to avoid an electrical shock, you have learned to smoke as a means of avoiding withdrawal symptoms or avoiding increased stress reactions.

19

Pavlov and his drooling dogs have taught us that behaviors can also be learned through pairing, or association, with other stimuli. Any smoker will tell you that "smoking relaxes me." If nicotine is a stimulant, how can it relax you? For years you have probably smoked while taking a work break, or while relaxing reading the newspaper. The pairing of the relaxation you experience from taking a break with smoking led you to psychologically learn that smoking is relaxing. While smoking for relaxation may be viewed as more socially acceptable than drooling, it may be easier to learn to be a non-drooler than a nonsmoker. (Please look for our next book "Salvation from Salivation: Doggy Drooling Cessation Program" coming soon to a bookstore near you).

Skinner and Pavlov also demonstrated that any behavior that is learned can be unlearned. By removing the pleasure resulting from the behavior, the behavior will be extinguished and fade. They also showed that while it can be difficult to extinguish a learned behavior, the behavior can easily return by being rewarded only once. Giving into *just one* cigarette can reinitiate the habit. Keep this in the back of your mind when we work on relapse prevention in weeks five and six.

Through years of associating smoking with various emotions and situations, smoking has become an automatic, learned habit. Before you identify why you are stressed or angry, you've already located your cigarettes, your lighter, and a cigarette is in your mouth. You now have to learn how to be a nonsmoker, and how to deal with stress, anger, or social interactions without cigarettes.

Self-Monitoring

There are many reasons that people smoke. In order to effectively quit smoking, you need to be aware of the people, situations, and emotions that are associated with your habitual behavior. One of the best ways to become aware of your smoking patterns is to write down the whens, whys, whos, and wheres of your smoking. This helps you to identify the reasons that you smoke and can also assist you in learning how to break some of these patterns.

Daily Cigarette Monitoring Forms can be found in the Appendix. You will be completing the forms for one whole week **without changing your smoking patterns.** This will allow you to identify patterns of smoking across a variety of situations. It will also heighten your self-awareness of your feelings, the relative importance of some cigarettes to others, and how you use cigarettes as a coping tool or a reward.

This one week period will enable you to monitor your cigarette use across five weekdays and the weekend. You may begin on any day of the week. It is important that you do not change your smoking habits during this first week. If you feel compelled to get an early jump on cutting down your nicotine consumption, you can butt your cigarette two puffs earlier than you would normally. We advise you against cutting down more than this, or switching to a low nicotine cigarette, because you will likely smoke more often in response to cravings. This will result in a misrepresentation of your actual habits.

To use the Daily Cigarette Monitoring Form:

- Photocopy the Monitoring Forms back to back on paper (preferably colored paper, to make it easier to locate). Each page will enable you to monitor four packs, so make enough double sided copies to cover 28 days (seven days x four weeks).

- Cut each of the pages into quarters. Each quarter should consist of one form with numbers, ranging from 1-10 on the front, and 11-20 on the back. Each number corresponds to a cigarette in a pack (for the rocket scientists in the crowd: 1 Form=1 Pack). Keep this form and a pen in the plastic sleeve of your cigarette pack. This way, it will be immediately available to fill in.

- Write down the *Time* , *Activity* or *Place* , *Who* you are with, and your *Mood* or *Reason* for smoking.

- Rate the importance, or level of *Need* , in the third column. 1= least needed cigarette, 10= most needed. For example: At 8:15 a.m. you had your third cigarette while driving to work alone. You were feeling tense because of heavy traffic. You felt a moderate need for this cigarette.

#	Time	Need	Activity or Place	With Whom	Mood or Reason
3	8:15 AM	6	in car going to work	alone	Tense-heavy traffic

Be as accurate as possible. Do not wait until the end of the day to write down your recollections of each cigarette. It is important to stop and determine the specific factors associated with each cigarette *as you smoke it.*

Weaning Down vs. "Cold Turkey"

By now you are aware that dependency on cigarettes is twofold: behavioral and physical. The learned behavioral response of smoking, which includes habit and a strong emotional component, were just discussed. Of equal difficulty for many people is the breaking the physical dependency, or addiction, to nicotine.

The most common withdrawal symptoms include:

- irritability

- dizziness/lightheadedness

- nervousness

- shakiness

- headaches

- difficulty concentrating

- shortness of breath

- sweating

- disrupted sleep

- heart palpitations

- feeling lethargic

You may feel some, all, or none of these withdrawal symptoms when you begin to quit smoking. These are difficult feelings to ignore. Because the discomfort of withdrawal can be temporarily terminated by smoking a single cigarette, you may feel tempted to stop your "suffering" by slipping back into old habits. These temptations may be reduced or eliminated with the use of Nicotine replacement therapy (nicotine patch or gum), or with bupropion (Wellbutrin™ or Zyban™).

Through this program you will learn how to reinterpret these symptoms as symptoms of recovery. You will also learn how to identify and challenge your rationalizations for smoking in response to these feelings. Remember these feelings typically diminish after four weeks.

Some people find it easier to cut down on cigarettes over a period of weeks, while others prefer to quit completely at once ("cold turkey"). There are pros and cons to each process. Which one will be effective for you will be dependent on your habits, the amount that you smoke, and your reasons for smoking. It also depends on whether the physical addiction or the psychological/behavioral dependency is most difficult for you to break. Pros and cons of each method include:

Weaning Down

- Eliminating a proportion of your cigarette consumption can be a more comfortable process because it allows you to substitute alternative behaviors, while minimizing withdrawal symptoms.

- Cutting down allows you to learn new coping skills while controlling the physical symptoms of withdrawal.

Cold Turkey

- Quitting all at once allows you to make a "clean break," forcing you to make dramatic and immediate lifestyle changes.

- Quitting cold turkey is faster and allows you to become a nonsmoker earlier.

- Quitting cold turkey may lead to increased physical symptoms of withdrawal, unless done in conjunction with Nicotine replacement therapy (nicotine patch or gum) or bupropion (Wellbutrin or Zyban).

Whichever method you choose, Don't switch to low tar/nicotine cigarettes!

The Patch or Not the Patch: That is the Question...

Nicotine replacement therapy (nicotine patch, gum, nasal spray or inhaler) may be helpful in reducing or eliminating physical symptoms, allowing you to first address the behavioral and emotional components of smoking. They allow you to continue receiving nicotine, the stimulant present in cigarettes, without the harmful tar and carbon monoxide present in smoke. Nicotine replacement delivers nicotine into the bloodstream more slowly than smoking. It also delivers a lower dose of nicotine. All methods allow you to reduce the amount of nicotine you are absorbing, allowing you to slowly wean down on nicotine intake. Nicotine gum and patches have recently become available to the public over-the-counter without a prescription. Nicotine inhalers and nasal spray are available only by a doctor's prescription.

Benefits of Nicotine Replacement

Nicotine replacement therapy allows you to master one aspect of smoking cessation at a time. By alleviating withdrawal effects associated with quitting, it allows you to focus on changing your smoking behaviors and breaking your habits while eliminating the aforementioned withdrawal symptoms. Once you have gained control over the habitual aspects of smoking, you can begin to wean off, or completely stop the nicotine replacement (depending on the dosage of the nicotine). At the time that you are ready to do this (approximately 6-12 weeks after completely quitting cigarettes), you should have broken your habits, and replaced them with healthier, more appropriate means of coping. You will also experience increased self-efficacy (your own ability to effect change), which may make you feel stronger and better able to resist temptations resulting from withdrawal symptoms.

While nicotine patches, nasal spray and gum only address the physical withdrawal aspects associated with smoking, only the nicotine inhaler aids in both the physical and psychological aspects of quitting smoking. Nicotine inhalers are comprised of a mouthpiece and a nicotine-filled cartridge. Smokers breathe through the cigarette-sized device, inhaling approximately 30% of the nicotine found in a cigarette. Since the inhaler resembles a cigarette, the smoker can engage in, and experience some of the same behavioral patterns they would if they were smoking, without the harmful tar or carcinogens.

The Down Side of Nicotine Replacement

There are several negatives associated with nicotine replacement. The most obvious is that it prolongs the quitting process. Most nicotine replacement plans range in duration anywhere from 6-12 weeks. Once the behavioral dependency is successfully extinguished, the physical addiction must still be addressed. If you have difficulty tolerating the withdrawal symptoms, you may relapse, even after many successful weeks of not smoking.

It is imperative that the dosage of the replacement product is appropriate for your body weight and level of cigarette consumption. Some individuals believe that if they take a stronger dose than they normally acquire through smoking, they will be more successful because they have eliminated physical temptations. This is really a step backwards, because you now need to decrease your addiction to this higher level of nicotine. Most smokers should begin with a full strength patch for the first four weeks, then reduce to a lower strength for another 4-6 weeks.

Like any drug, nicotine replacement has potential side effects. Dizziness, heart palpitations, nausea, vomiting, disrupted sleep and headache are among the most common side effects. Potential side effects should be listed on the product container. Smokers who have heart disease or are pregnant should consult their physician before using any of these products.

The patch or gum can *only* be used when you *stop* smoking. If you have been systematically reducing your cigarette intake, be sure that you begin with a nicotine dosage that is equal to, or less than your most recent daily intake of cigarette consumption. Again, you don't want to go backwards.

Cost is another factor. For example, the average cost of the most common nicotine patches (Nicotrol™ and Nicoderm™) is approximately $30.00 per week. A 6 week, one step patch plan costs approximately $180.00. A three step plan lasting twelve weeks will cost you approximately double. A twelve week step-down nicotine gum program costs approximately $250.00. These programs do provide materials and audio tapes to address the behavioral aspects of quitting. Remember, if successful, the cost of these programs will quickly be recovered by your savings on cigarettes. In fact, the daily cost of the nicotine replacement products is approximately the same as the cost of smoking one pack of cigarettes per day.

Nicotine replacement is most effective for those who experience significant withdrawal symptoms, or for those who are heavy smokers. Reflect on your past attempts to quit.

Questions to Ask Yourself:

- What has been the most challenging part of quitting?

- What were the physical symptoms that you experienced?

- Which was more difficult for you to break, the physical or the psychological/behavioral dependency on cigarettes?

- If you were successful in becoming a nonsmoker and remaining a nonsmoker for over 30 days, what led you to relapse back into smoking? (Hint: if you remained a nonsmoker for over 30 days without nicotine replacement, you successfully broke the the physical addiction).

Based on your answers to these questions, you can determine whether nicotine replacement will be appropriate for you. If you decide to use the patch, inhaler or gum, you can quit smoking "cold turkey." Be sure to follow the directions for the product. **DO NOT SMOKE WHILE USING THE NICOTINE PATCH OR GUM.** Nicotine is a drug. A powerful drug. It is possible to overdose by using these products in conjunction with smoking. If you choose to utilize these products, be sure to closely follow the package directions.

Whether you decide to wean down or quit all at once, with or without nicotine replacement, **do not** change your smoking habits over the next week. Monitor your *current habits* on the daily monitoring form. This is important data that is essential for you to learn to identify and change your daily habits. Over the next week, decide whether weaning down or stopping "cold turkey" is most appropriate for you. Then, if you choose to eliminate smoking and begin with nicotine replacement, you can begin at the start of week two. If you feel that weaning down is more appropriate for you, your cigarette intake will be partially decreased at the beginning of next week.

Bupropion: Wellbutrin™ and Zyban™

Bupropion has recently been approved by the FDA as a nicotine-free substance for smoking cessation. This non-nicotine prescription medicine was initially distributed as an antidepressant under the name of Wellbutrin™. Zyban™ is the same medication marketed specifically for smoking cessation. Bupropion decreases cravings and withdrawal symptoms, as well as decreasing the desire to smoke. While it is unclear exactly how this medication works, it is believed to act on the part of the brain that is addicted to nicotine (Glaxowellcome, 2003).

In one large trial, quit rates for Bupropion were greater for than those using nicotine patches (Hyder Ferry, 1999). It can also be used safely in conjunction with the nicotine patch. Treatment with sustained release bupropion alone or in combination with a nicotine patch resulted in better long-term rates of smoking cessation than the use of the nicotine patch alone or placebo (Jorenby, 1999).

Unlike nicotine-replacement methods, bupropion does not contain nicotine. You reduce the amount of nicotine in your body by reducing your smoking. Nicotine patches and gums, on the other hand, directly administer nicotine to the body, but in a *alternative* form of nicotine that is safer than cigarettes. This is an important distinction for individuals who need to reduce their nicotine immediately, or who don't want to withdraw later from the nicotine replacement. Bupropion can also be used while smoking. In fact, medical guidelines recommend that smokers should set a quit date 10 days to two weeks after beginning bupropion (Hyder Ferry, 1999).

Because this medication takes time to build up in the blood stream, this allows for the medication to reach a therapeutic level prior to beginning the quitting process. Whether you choose to wean down or quit "cold turkey," you should begin taking the Buproprion as soon as possible. This will allow it to approach a therapeutic dose in the blood system soon after the beginning of week 2.

Bupropion is available only through a prescription. The typical starting dose is 150 mg. per day for three to five days, and then increase, for most patients, to the maximum dose of 300 mg. per day (150 mg. taken twice daily). Once you quit smoking, continue on the medication until your doctor tells you to discontinue it. Common side effects include dry mouth and difficulty sleeping. As with any medication, there are certain risks, so it is important to speak to your health care provider to determine whether this medication is right for you.

Despite highly published success rates for nicotine replacement therapies and medications, the long-term success rate is higher when used in combination with behavioral techniques. Good stress management techniques are necessary to remain a lifelong nonsmoker!

- Review of Self-Monitoring Sheets

- Fears of Quitting

- Rewards

- Begin Now!

This chapter will allow you to better understand yourself and your patterns of behaviors and emotions associated with smoking. It will assist you in identifying your smoking patterns and habits, recognizing and challenging your fears about quitting and selecting short-term and long-term rewards. In addition, you will begin to reduce your smoking by one-third (or completely, if you choose to quit "cold turkey.")

Review of Self-Monitoring Sheets

For the past week you have been paying close attention to your smoking patterns. Take out your Cigarette Monitoring Forms and study them closely, looking for patterns such as people or places and situations frequently associated with smoking. Next look at the reasons or your mood at the time you chose to smoke. Lastly, identify those variables associated with the cigarettes you deemed as "most important" (8-10 on the 10 point scale).

Write down the answers following questions about your smoking habits:

1) The most common places that I smoke are:

2) The most frequent times that I smoke are:

3) The people I most often smoke with are:

4) I tend to smoke the most when I am feeling:

5) The most common reasons I smoke are:

6) The times and reasons associated with the most needed cigarettes are:

7) For me, the situations that are going to be the hardest to be without cigarettes are:

Fears of Quitting

Smoking has provided you with many years of comfort and pleasure. For many people, cigarettes have become a reliable friend, a sense of security. Whenever we make changes in our life we may begin to feel a sense of fear or insecurity. Just as you would feel hesitant and scared to give up a long-term relationship with a close friend or companion, you may feel scared about giving up cigarettes. There are many common fears associated with smoking cessation, including the fear of weight gain, being able to cope with stress, feeling isolated from your smoking friends, being "too grouchy" around your partner, or the fear of failure if once again you don't quit. It is important to identify your fears so you can effectively challenge them. If you don't challenge these fears, you will begin to rationalize returning to smoking.

Identify and write down your fears about quitting smoking in the left hand column:

Fear	Rational?	Challenge to Rationalization
	☐ Rational ☐ Irrational	
	☐ Rational ☐ Irrational	
	☐ Rational ☐ Irrational	
	☐ Rational ☐ Irrational	

Now go through this list and note in the middle column whether this is a *rational* fear, or an *irrational* fear. For example, fear of weight gain is a rational fear, as most people gain an average of five to ten pounds within months of quitting cigarettes. Fear that your husband will find you to be so grouchy that he will shave his head, put on a leather thong, and run away to join a cult of burned out Trekies in search of the Energizer Bunny is irrational. (If you feel this is a rational possibility, please, don't put your energy into smoking cessation. You have bigger problems to face. Make sure that your medical insurance has good mental health coverage!)

In the right hand column, write down your *challenges* to these fears. For example, "I don't have to gain weight if I watch my eating habits or if I exercise more." or "Bob will understand that I will be irritable, and it is only temporary."

If you are having difficulty challenging your fears, feel free to consult a close friend, or ask for some help from someone who has successfully quit.

Over the next month, pay close attention to your fears or rationalizations. If you begin to rationalize these fears, you must immediately stop them and challenge them. Return to the list of reasons for quitting that you wrote in Week 1. Remind yourself over and over, until the fears dissipate, or until you can view them as irrational. This is referred to as *self-talk.* We will discuss self-talk in more detail in later weeks.

Rewards

Last week we discussed Operant and Classical Conditioning. Remember Pavlov and his dogs (that name should ring a bell)? Operant Conditioning demonstrates that behavior which is rewarded is more likely to be repeated than behavior which is not rewarded. At one time, past or present, smoking was pleasurable and rewarding for you. Now you may feel that you are depriving yourself. You are giving up something that has been comforting or enjoyable for many years.

You need to replace that loss of pleasure in your life to increase the likelihood that you will continue to be a nonsmoker. You need to reward yourself for your efforts. Quitting is not easy, and requires self-discipline. For many, self-discipline equals deprivation. If you feel that you are depriving yourself of all pleasure, you will begin to feel more like a victim than a victor. You need to feel in control, and you need to replace some of that lost pleasure with other pleasures.

Rewards need to be immediate, frequent, and pleasurable in order to reinforce your quitting behaviors. While the reward for quitting may be an extra ten years of life, you shouldn't have to wait another twenty-five years to experience the reward (besides, when you're seventy-three, how do you know that you are getting the next ten years as a bonus for quitting? It's not like we come with a visible termination date that can be upgraded by showing that you made positive changes in your life.) For this reason, you must identify short term as well as long-term rewards. They must be realistic rewards that can be enjoyed at that time.

Next, list rewards for each of the weeks that you are successful in quitting. Remember, success is not necessarily "all or nothing." For instance, let's say that you were supposed to cut down by a third, from thirty cigarettes a day to twenty per day this week. On Thursday, you slipped and smoked twenty-two cigarettes because you and your spouse had a fight. Friday you evaluated your behavior and decided to stick with the program. You also decided to cut down another two cigarettes that day to make up for the slip. This is a success that should be rewarded. Just making the decision to pick yourself up by the bootstraps and continue with the program is a success.

Hint: If you listed weight gain as one of your fears, be sure to avoid food-related rewards. You may want to make a gym membership a reward. If you listed increased tension as a fear, a visit to the massage therapist (massage *therapist*, **not** massage *parlor*) would be a great reward. Remember to pick some rewards that will help to boost your self-esteem or that will be relaxing.

Week #	Reward
2	
3	
4	
5	
6	

Now identify long-term rewards for months 1-6 after your successful quit date. You should also reward yourself for your one year anniversary. Many people like to use the money they saved from not smoking for a year (about $1600/year for one-pack a day habit) to purchase something special or a vacation.

Month #	Reward
1	
2	
3	
4	
5	
6	
1 year!	

Begin Now!

If you have decided to follow the program through the weaning down process, you will begin this today. (All right, stop whining. You've had a whole week to mentally prepare yourself for this. This is it, no more excuses! If you're making up rationalizations already, examine your willingness to give up your habit at this time.)

Now go through the monitoring forms and identify the least needed cigarettes. Assuming that your smoking habits are fairly regular from day to day, these will be the first cigarettes that you should eliminate. Remember, the easier it is for you to succeed, the more you will succeed. The more you succeed, the more confidence you will have in yourself and your ability to quit. The more confidence you have in yourself, the easier it will be for you to quit and stay quit.

Cut down on your smoking by at least **one-third.** For example, if you regularly smoke a pack a day, you can only allow yourself 13 cigarettes per day (two-thirds of 20). Each day put only the number of cigarettes allowed in an empty pack and put the remainder out of reach. Having access to only those allowed can help you to budget your daily allotment and give you a visual cue as to how many you have left for the day. Having the remaining cigarettes out of reach also makes it more difficult to impulsively smoke extra, or to make rationalizations. Even if it sounds silly to count out your cigarettes for the day ahead of time and hide the rest from yourself, please just trust us and do it anyway.

Continue to complete the cigarette monitoring forms for each cigarette.

Hint: You can make it even more difficult by giving your extra cigarettes to a supportive other, or a quitting partner to hold. The anticipated embarrassment of asking for them back may be enough to dissuade you from smoking additional cigarettes. Be sure to explain to the supportive other what you expect from them (i.e., "If I ask for another one, talk me out of it" or "Don't give me any, no matter how long I grovel.")

Remember: If you do not already smoke them, do not switch to low tar/ low nicotine cigarettes. This often leads to increased smoking as a means of reducing withdrawal symptoms.

Stopping "Cold Turkey:" With or Without Nicotine Replacement Therapy

If you are opting to use Nicotine Replacement (gum or patch), you will also begin to stop smoking today. (No whining from you either.) Remember, you **cannot smoke** while using the nicotine replacement. Follow the directions on the package, and consult their toll free number, or your pharmacist if you have any questions.

Review *all* of the information presented in this and all of the upcoming units. You do not have to follow the instructions for cutting down, but the information regarding habits and behaviors *must* be followed to be successful. In future sections when we address withdrawal and physical symptoms, be sure to save this information. You will need to go back and address these issues when you begin to wean from the patch or gum. If you wish, you may also complete week three of the program this week, in addition to week 2.

Remember: **Be very nice to yourself** over the next few weeks. You are working hard and deserve to feel good. It is appropriate to reward yourself daily with smaller rewards for a job well done. Always give yourself a pat on the back for resisting temptation or for coping well with stress. If you feel that such acknowledgment from close friends or companions is very important to you, be sure to tell them what you need. Research demonstrates that good support significantly increases the likelihood of success.

Week Three: Coping with Stress

- Examining Your Progress

- Reduce by Another One-third

- Breaking Old Habits

- STRESSED is More Than DESSERTS Spelled Backwards

- Assessing your Current Coping Skills

- Increasing your Coping Skills

- Deep Breathing and Deep Muscle Relaxation Training

- Stop Smoking Contract

- Reward Yourself

Welcome to Week three of the Quit for Life program. Believe it or not, you're almost half way to being a nonsmoker if you are weaning down. Some of the hardest work is behind you. Take a moment to give yourself a pat on the back, and praise yourself for sticking with the program thus far. You should begin to feel more confident in your ability to successfully quit. By taking one day at a time, you will feel even more confident in your ability to cope and to live cigarette free.

Examining Your Progress

You may have faced some difficult times in cutting down your smoking in the past week. Review your Daily Cigarette Monitoring Forms for the past seven days. Did you comply with your limit (2/3 limit if weaning; zero cigarettes if going cold-turkey)? If you complied with the limit, congratulate yourself profusely. Relish in your success. If you exceeded your daily limit, you experienced what is called a "lapse" or a "slip." Take a moment (and only a moment) to punish yourself sufficiently, and move on. It is important not to continually focus on your slip and beat yourself up over it. This will do nothing positive. It will only diminish your confidence and lower your motivation to continue. It is more important for you to acknowledge your slip and continue working at the program.

If you had a slip, it is important to analyze the events and feelings that were present during that day. Answer and reflect upon the following questions:

1. What happened that led me to smoke additional cigarettes?

2. What was I feeling at the time?

3. Was this a typical event or feeling, or was it unexpected and took me by surprise?

4. What could I have said to myself (self-talk) to dissuade me from smoking?

5. What could I have done in this situation instead of smoking?

6. What have I learned from this situation?

If you had a slip, it is important to learn from this situation to help you to anticipate future "high-risk" situations and to develop a contingency backup plan to cope with these situations. Just like the seemingly useless fire drills in which you participated in grade school, you may have never had to evacuate the building, but it was important to have a plan about how to respond. This helped you to know how to respond in the event of a fire and build your confidence that you could handle the situation.

Let's look at the following example: "Last week I had two extra cigarettes because I felt tense when we visited my in-laws for dinner."

Step One: *Identify high risk situation:* In-laws = stress.

Step Two: *What was I feeling at the time?* I was feeling tense, bored, and irritated.

Step Three: *Was this a typical event or feeling, or was it unexpected?* It was typical, we go over there every weekend. I should have anticipated the tension, because it has been the same experience every week for twelve years.

Step Four: *What could I have said to myself to dissuade me from smoking?* I should have reminded myself that I can handle the stress, and that smoking only adds to the anxiety by dumping stimulants into my body. I could think that I wouldn't give my in-laws the satisfaction of dying twenty years early from a heart attack. I could have told myself that I would only be hurting myself by smoking an additional cigarette. I should have reminded myself how well I have done, and allowed myself to feel proud, rather than irritated.

Step Five: *What could I have done instead of smoking?* When I began to feel tense, I should have excused myself, gone out for a breath of fresh air and did some deep breathing exercises. I could have brought some gum to chew.

Step Six: *What have I learned from this situation?* To be prepared to deal with the typical tension or boredom. Don't bring extra cigarettes with me to their house. Bring candy or gum as a substitute. (Next time I get married I will check out my fiancé's family before saying "I do.")

Now, take a minute to review your list of fears from week two. If you had a slip, how often did you rationalize your behavior through these fears? (If your spouse *did* set off in search of that long-eared pink rodent with the drum, please be sure to send a picture of his bald head and leather thong. We'll be happy to give you an appropriate psychiatric referral.)

Reduce by Another One-Third

If you are weaning down, the time has come to take the next step: Reduction of your daily cigarette intake by another one-third. This should be one-third of the original amount (not one-third of last week's allotment--nice try!) Follow the same process of examining your patterns, and eliminating those cigarettes with the lowest ranking of "need." For most smokers, the first and last cigarette of the day are the most needed, in part due to habit, and also from physical dependence. The first cigarette of the morning is likely the one with the strongest physical craving, because your body has been deprived of nicotine for the previous eight hours.

Once again, look for patterns such as the people, places and situations most frequently associated with smoking. Look at the reasons or your mood at the time you chose to smoke. Identify the factors associated with the cigarettes you rated as "most important" (8-10 on the 10 point scale).

Answer and Reflect on the following questions:

What are the most common feelings that lead me to smoke?

The most common reasons I smoke are:

I plan to eliminate these cigarettes:

The situations that are going to be the hardest for me to go without cigarettes this week are:

My plan to cope with these situations is:

Breaking Old Habits

In Week One, we discussed how habits are developed through conditioning. You now need to learn to de-condition yourself from your smoking habits. This can be accomplished by interrupting or breaking the coupling of smoking with other behaviors or places. For instance, when we go to the theater to watch a movie, what is the first food we think of? Popcorn. Some people cannot watch a movie at the theater without munching on popcorn. Why? Because we are conditioned: Movie = Popcorn. Some of these same people, however, never consider having popcorn while watching a movie in their own living room. The same is true for cigarettes. Now the psychologist in these authors comes out. Please free associate and answer the first word that comes to your mind:

Morning coffee and _____ *(hint: the correct answer is cigarette)*

Dessert, coffee, and _____

Coffee break and _____

Driving in the car and _____

Bedtime and _____

Stress and _____

You get the idea. You have already identified your typical situations associated with smoking. Your next step in breaking these associations is to insert barriers into these situations. For example, many offices and government buildings now prohibit smoking. These barriers have forced many people to cut down their daily smoking by forbidding smoking in the workplace. Those who are desperate enough will find

54

themselves standing out in the cold rain to feed their addiction. This barrier has forced them to smoke only at certain times and makes it so inconvenient that you have to go out of your way to have that cigarette. Sometimes its not worth the hassle, so a smoker chooses to wait until after work to enjoy their cigarette.

Change daily habits that are associated with smoking, such as:

- Leaving the table immediately after a meal, to avoid the dessert-coffee-cigarette association.
- Sit in a different chair at the dining room table, or in the living room.
- Read or use relaxation techniques to relax your mind before falling asleep.
- Use the hot shower as soon as you wake up, rather than nicotine, to stimulate you in the morning.
- Go for a walk, read a book, or do relaxation techniques during coffee breaks or immediately after lunch.
- Do not hang around the staff lounge if that is a place where you used to smoke or others continue to smoke.
- Make up barriers, including rules, that will make it extra difficult for you to smoke that cigarette. Here are some examples:
  - No smoking in bed (for safety reasons, this should be a universal rule).
  - No smoking in the bedroom, or even better, in the house.
  - Smoke only in the most uncomfortable room in the house (e.g., bathroom or basement).
  - Require five minutes of exercise before each cigarette.

- Make smoking contingent upon completion of an undesirable chore.

- No smoking in the car.

- Never have a cigarette with a cup of coffee or an alcoholic beverage.

- Keep your cigarettes in your car trunk.

- Ask someone else to hold your cigarettes, so you need to ask for each one, rather than grabbing them without awareness.

Make it even harder on yourself by posting these rules or informing your supportive friends or family. This creates social pressure to adhere to your own rules. If you have the money, have your car's interior detailed, so you won't want to smell it up, or burn the upholstery. Have your draperies cleaned when you decide to outlaw smoking in the house. Most importantly, request that others respect the same rules as a supportive measure.

Face it: If you want a cigarette badly enough, you'll go out to your car trunk in the middle of the night and smoke it in the garage, per your rules. Providing that these cigarettes are allotted in your day, it is OK. This technique makes you stop, think, and make the decision as to whether you want that cigarette badly enough to inconvenience yourself. It also assists you in deconditioning your connection between smoking and certain places or engaging in certain behaviors. For those of you who were amazed at how many cigarettes you smoked without being aware, this technique will help you to be more conscious of your decisions to smoke.

I plan to make the following changes in my smoking habits this week:

_____

_____

_____

_____

STRESSED is More Than DESSERTS Spelled Backwards

Stress is a complex and uncomfortable entity that penetrates our lives on a daily basis. There is an old saying that nothing in life is sure except death and taxes. That is the abridged version. The truth is that nothing in life is sure except death, *stress* and taxes. Anybody who has endured graduate school or child rearing can vouch for this.

One factor that influences the amount of stress perceived is whether the situation is controllable. If we have control over a situation, it tends to be less stressful than if we have no control over it. Control implies power, or the ability to influence the outcome of the situation. Without control, we often feel helpless or victimized. Unfortunately, we cannot control all of the factors in our lives. Our clients get tired of us saying "If you can't control the stressful situation control your reactions to it." Stress is inevitable. Do your best to control the factors in your life that are stressful. If you cannot control a situation, control your reaction to it. For example, imagine that you are stuck in traffic and are late for an important appointment. You begin to feel tense and anxious. Examine the situation. Is there anything you can do to change or control the situation? There are no alternative routes and no way to contact your client to tell her that you will be late. You reach for your cigarettes as if you are thinking "I'm not anxious enough. What I could use is some extra stimulants in my nervous system right now." So you arrive to your appointment 45 minutes late, shaking, sweating, and reeking of tobacco. You are are even more upset because you've been working so hard to stop smoking. You're angry at yourself, the person who caused the car accident and resulting traffic jam (which they probably did just to inconvenience you), and you have a headache or stomach ache from the stress.

If you cannot control the situation, control your reaction to it. By using deep breathing techniques, self-talk (e.g. saying to yourself "There is nothing I can do about this, and getting upset doesn't make it any better") or listening to calming music you can control your reactions to the situation. You will still arrive 45 minutes late, but without a headache, tight muscles, or nervousness.

In moderate amounts, stress can be motivating. It is the only thing that gets people to complete their income tax by 11:59 P.M. on April 15 of each year. In large amounts, stress can be debilitating and paralyzing, interfering with your ability to reach your goal. (That's why these authors found it easier to work three jobs, have children, and put an addition on a house rather than focus on completing their Doctoral Dissertations in a timely fashion).

Why is it that some individuals can withstand the stress of Medical school, surviving on Ramen Noodles and Kraft Macaroni and cheese, while being stranded in their 1978 Volare on the way to the divorce attorney, while others become devastated and begin to decompensate when their laser printer runs out of toner? Obviously, there are many factors that determines one's ability to withstand stress. Assuming that one is of sound mind and body, the key factor is: The ability to cope.

We do not deny that there may be unexpected stressors with which you weren't prepared to cope. The questions you must ask yourself is: "How did having a cigarette help me cope with or resolve the problem?" Let us guess. "It helped me to calm down so that I could think clearly enough to solve the problem." Remove the rationalization from this statement and it translates into "The infiltration of carbon monoxide into my blood restricted the amount of oxygen to my brain which helped me to think more clearly." Unless you're half Vulcan, reduced oxygen to the brain impairs your ability to think more clearly. (Note: If you are half Vulcan, there is no need to complete the "mood" portion of the Cigarette Monitoring Form).

The underlying message to that rationalization is that you tend to rely on cigarettes to help you calm down and cope. Therefore, being unable to cope with stress becomes a common fear. How then, do nonsmokers cope with stress? They use other coping strategies to help them cope and to reduce their stress.

Assessing your Current Coping Skills

There is no need to tell you what stress is. You know. What you may not know is what stress means to you personally. Everybody differs in what they perceive to be stressful. The word "perceive" is an important one. It is not necessarily the event, but how you perceive that event that dictates how much stress you feel. For example, the perception that one will be laid off in a company downsizing is extremely stressful. One does not have to wait until they have a pink slip in hand before they begin to worry or feel stressed. It may not happen, but the threat or perceived threat is there, resulting in stress.

In addition, the way in which one perceives an event will determine how much stress they feel. A perfect example is the conception of a baby. For a couple that has struggled with infertility for many years, conception of a child is a happy and blessed event. Remember, any change, even positive change, is stressful. This same event, however, will be significantly more stressful for a teenage girl who accidentally conceived and is faced with telling her parents.

It is important to identify the typical stressors in your life. While most people share some of the same stressors, we all tend to have our own "hot spots." For example, financial issues, colleagues at work, getting stuck in traffic, civil injustice, etc.

Complete the following:

The things that "stress me out" the most are:

_____

_____

_____

_____

_____

_____

_____

_____

Everybody reacts to stress differently. How you feel in response to stress will differ from the way in which your partner or your best friend responds to stress. However, we tend to react to stress the same way within ourselves. For example, in nine out of ten stressful situations you may feel overwhelmed, perspire excessively, have heart palpitations and difficulty concentrating. Nine out of ten times, another person will have tightened muscles, feel fatigued, experience a headache, and lose his appetite when faced with stress.

To better cope with stress, you need to be aware of your reactions to stress. Think about a typical stressful situation.

Check the emotional reactions you most often have when faced with this, or any, stressful situation:

☐ Irritable/edgy

☐ Anxious

☐ Depressed

☐ Angry

☐ Difficulty making decisions

☐ Can't concentrate

☐ Short-tempered

☐ Feel ineffective

☐ Overwhelmed

☐ Tense

☐ Drained

☐ Lack confidence

☐ Frustrated

☐ Feel badly about myself

☐ Guilty

☐ Others: _____

When faced with stress, which of these physical symptoms do you experience:

- ☐ Increased heart rate
- ☐ Increased blood pressure
- ☐ Fatigue
- ☐ Gastrointestinal problems
- ☐ Heart palpitations
- ☐ Sweating
- ☐ Loss of appetite
- ☐ Rash/hives
- ☐ Chest pains
- ☐ Others: _____

- ☐ Accelerated breathing
- ☐ Stomach ache
- ☐ Inability to sleep
- ☐ Sleep too much
- ☐ Shaking
- ☐ Tense muscles
- ☐ Diarrhea
- ☐ Panic attacks
- ☐ Shortness of breath

_____ _____

There are numerous coping skills available. As creatures of habit, we tend to utilize the same few techniques whenever we are faced with stress. It's like choosing the same three tools from a full toolbox every time you need to repair something. While a hammer, screwdriver, and wrench may be the appropriate tools for some repairs, they are unsuitable for others. Having a limited set of coping tools is much like having a limited set of hand tools. Sometimes the tools you have are too limited, and therefore inappropriate for the task. Using a screwdriver and a hammer as a substitute for a chisel may get the job done, but it is likely going to be less effective than using the correct tool (and ruin the screwdriver in the process).

First, take a moment to assess the coping tools you have in your "toolbox." Some are appropriate coping skills, and others are inappropriate, but are commonly used nonetheless.

Check off the coping tools or techniques that you use most often:

- ☐ Talk to others/use support
- ☐ Pray
- ☐ Use relaxation or meditation
- ☐ Talk to myself (self-talk)
- ☐ Seek more information
- ☐ Escape the situation
- ☐ Ignore the situation
- ☐ Socially withdraw
- ☐ Smoke
- ☐ Make a list of options
- ☐ Complain
- ☐ Explode/become aggressive
- ☐ Use deep breathing
- ☐ Other: _____
- ☐ Other: _____

- ☐ Distract myself/keep busy
- ☐ Think about the possible solutions
- ☐ Look for the silver lining
- ☐ Exercise/physically release tension
- ☐ Drink alcohol
- ☐ Let someone else handle it
- ☐ Tell myself "things could be worse"
- ☐ Abuse medications or drugs
- ☐ Ask others how they would handle it
- ☐ Eat
- ☐ Be assertive
- ☐ Act without thinking things through
- ☐ Try to see the other's point of view
- ☐ Other: _____
- ☐ Other: _____

How you choose to cope is often contingent upon the situation and the consequences of the situation. One reason for using a limited number of coping skills is that we have learned to feel comfortable with the skills we have used in the past. This may be that we have found a set of techniques that have served us well and have benefited us. It may also be that we are afraid of learning how to use a new technique. Nobody wants to try something new, especially when under stress and feeling physical or emotional discomfort. Perhaps that is why you may have listed "inability to handle stress" when asked to list your fears of giving up cigarettes in Week Two.

Go through the list of stressors you wrote earlier in this chapter and indicate with a star which of these you have some control over. Indicate what you can do to control these situations so that you can eliminate or minimize the stress you feel.

Next to those items that you feel you cannot control, write down a coping technique that can help you control your reaction to event. Let's return to the example of getting stuck in traffic. Can I control this by getting off at the next exit and using an alternative route? If not, then I must control my reactions to it. I can put some relaxing music on the radio, mentally make up my "to do list," do some deep breathing and engage in self-talk. Things you can say to yourself are: "I'm stuck in traffic, and I will be 45 minutes late. I can either arrive to my destination 45 minutes late feeling tense, angry, and have a tension headache, or I can arrive 45 minutes late feeling none of those." Getting tense and angry is not going to relieve the traffic jam. Again, if you cannot control the event, control your reactions to it. If you were really smart, you would locked your cigarettes in the trunk, so that you couldn't possibly smoke them if you wanted to.

As you recall, everybody reacts to stress differently. Your reaction to stress, both physically and emotionally, differs among individuals, but is consistent within yourself. The same is generally true for how we cope with stress. Everybody copes differently, but tends to be consistent within themselves.

Increasing Your Coping Skills

Everyone could benefit from expanding their stress management "toolbox." Over the course of the next few weeks, you will be taught about some of the most effective coping techniques. If they are not already part of your coping repertoire, they should be learned and integrated into your current set of skills. These techniques will not only be useful for conquering smoking, but are essential in effectively dealing with the stress that is inevitable at home or work.

Possessing good coping skills also contributes to a sense of confidence and self-esteem. You may not need to use these skills on a daily basis, but the more often you successfully handle a stressful situation, the more confident you will likely be in the future when faced with the same or similar situations.

This week you will learn two valuable stress management techniques: Deep Breathing and Deep Muscle Relaxation Training. In weeks five and six, you will learn other important skills such as Positive Self-talk and Anticipating High Risk Situations. In the meantime, go back over the Coping techniques checklist, and think how you might begin to integrate some of the more self-explanatory positive coping skills into your daily life.

Deep Breathing and Deep Muscle Relaxation Training

When you feel any type of anxiety or discomfort, your body automatically responds. You may notice your heart beating faster, your muscles tightening up, and your breathing accelerate. This makes it harder to focus, think clearly, and use good problem solving skills. In the past, you would reach for a cigarette to help reduce this tension. One reason you may have felt more relaxed is that when smoking you inhaled deeply to get the fullest impact of the tobacco. Although you weren't getting pure oxygen with each deep breath, the act of breathing deeper and slower reduces muscle tension, and helps to distract you from the stressful situation.

Relaxation training incorporates slow deep breathing with deep relaxation of all of the muscles in the body. This is one of the most beneficial stress management tools available. Once learned, it can be used almost anywhere (with the exception of driving and operating heavy machinery), and can be extremely effective in reducing both physical and emotional tension. Deep breathing can be used alone, or in conjunction with relaxation.

Deep Breathing

Begin by slowly and deeply breathing in through your nose, and out through your mouth. Allow yourself to breathe from your diaphragm (the muscles under your ribcage). Place your hand on your stomach, just below the rib cage. When you breathe with your diaphragm, your hand will rise and drop with each breath. Avoid breathing too quickly, or taking shallow breaths from the chest. Inhale slowly to the count of four. Hold for 1 second. Exhale to the count of five. Breathe slowly and evenly. Remember, if you breathe too quickly, you will hyperventilate.

Do this for several breaths. Now enhance the effectiveness by adding positive self-talk, telling yourself "Relax" or "I can handle this."

Progressive Muscle Relaxation

Progressive Muscle Relaxation is one of the most common types of deep muscle relaxation. It allows you to systematically tense and relax each major muscle group in the body. When you tense each muscle, as described below, hold it tightly for 8-10 seconds. The muscle may begin to shake. Let go abruptly, allowing the muscle to feel limp like a rag doll. Repeat. While tensing each muscle group, remember to keep the rest of the body relaxed. You will tighten and relax each major muscle group twice. If you have pain or physical problems that create more discomfort by tensing that muscle (e.g., back problems, TMJ), DO NOT tense that specific muscle group. Instead, focus on releasing the tension from that muscle, allowing it to relax.

1. Begin by finding a quiet, comfortable place, where you will be undisturbed for 15 minutes.

2. Find a comfortable position. You may close your eyes if you choose.

3. Begin to slowly and deeply breathe from your diaphragm. Continue to focus on your breathing, while you begin to relax your whole body.

4. With your right hand, make a fist. Hold for 8-10 seconds then release. Repeat.

5. Make a fist with your left hand. Hold, then release. Repeat.

6. Tense your forehead by either raising your eyebrows, or squinting your eyes. Hold, then release. Repeat.

7. Clench your teeth. Feel the tension in your jaw. Hold, then release. Repeat.

8. Shrug your shoulders, lifting them up to your ears. Hold, then release. Repeat.

9. Tighten your stomach muscles and tighten your lower back. Hold, release. Repeat.

10. Squeeze your buttocks together. Hold, then release. Repeat.

11. Tighten both thighs. Hold, release. Repeat.

12. Tighten the calves of both legs. Hold, then release. Repeat.

13. Curl your toes. Hold, then release. Repeat.

14. Allow your entire body to "let go" even further, allowing all of the tension to leave your body. Continue to breathe slowly and deeply.

15. When you are ready, return your awareness back into the room around you. Slowly stretch and enjoy the feelings of relaxation.

This procedure is easy to learn, but it takes practice. Sometimes the use of soft relaxing music can enhance the feelings of relaxation.

Other types of relaxation, including "Guided Imagery" are also very effective for receiving deep relaxation. It can be difficult to learn on your own, if you haven't had experience with relaxation before. If you are having difficulty following the relaxation procedure on your own, relaxation tapes can be purchased at your local bookstore or nature emporium. They typically range in price from $17.00-$30.00. A tape can be also be purchased directly through our web site: http://interpersonalnet.com/quitforlife/ for $11.95 + $3.95 shipping and handling ($15.90 total plus tax). It contains both the Progressive Muscle Relaxation procedure and a smoking cessation Hypnosis Induction (which will be discussed in the next chapter). You actually receive two taped procedures for less than the typical price of one.

Stop Smoking Contract

This week, you will complete a stop smoking contract, if you are weaning down. It is your way of showing your commitment to quit. Choose a date approximately one week from today. This will allow you seven full days to finish the weaning process. On your designated quit day, read the Week Four chapter for further instructions and assistance.

The Stop Smoking Contract is located in the Appendix. Select a Quit date for next week and complete the contract. Sign it in front of your supportive friends or family members. If one of your reasons for quitting is for the benefit of your family, you may want to have your children sign it as "witnesses." This also adds to your feeling of accountability to your family.

Throw out, or give away, *all of your cigarettes, your ashtrays, and your lighters.* Yes, even your favorite, lucky lighter. Don't play mind games by hiding one pack of cigarettes "just in case." You want to make it as difficult as possible for you to return to smoking.

Reward Yourself

Last week you selected a reward for this past week. Give yourself that reward if you feel that you have been successful. Remember, success is not necessarily "all or nothing." If you had a slip, making the commitment to continue with the program is considered success.

Continue to be extra nice to yourself over the next few weeks. You are working hard and deserve to feel good. It is appropriate to reward yourself daily with smaller rewards for a job well done. Always give yourself a pat on the back for resisting temptation or for coping well.

Week Four: Quit Today

- Reviewing Your Progress

- Hypnosis

- Quit Today!

- Understanding How your Body is Already Repairing Itself: Withdrawal Effects

- Fighting Cravings and Urges

- Identifying Alternative Pleasurable Activities

- Avoiding Weight Gain

Without a doubt, Week 4 of the Quit for Life program is the most important week. By the end of this week, you will have attained official status as a nonsmoker, and will have survived most of the nicotine cravings and other withdrawal symptoms. For many, this week is the the most challenging, however, it is certainly the most rewarding.

Last week you agreed to a stop smoking contract. You chose a quit date and signed the contract in front of a supportive witness. Beginning today, your quit date, you will stop smoking completely. You will also learn about the use of hypnosis in quitting and abstaining, learn additional coping skills, address weight-gain concerns, reconceptualize cravings, and understand how your body is already repairing itself.

Reviewing Your Progress

First, lets take a few minutes to review this past week. Review your Daily Cigarette Monitoring Forms for the past seven days. Did you comply with the 1/3 limit? If you were successful, congratulate yourself. Enjoy your success. If you exceeded your daily limit, you experienced a *lapse* or a *slip*. Do not continually focus on your slip and beat yourself up over it. This will only decrease your self-confidence and motivation, which lowers your chances of success. It is more important for you to learn from your slip, and continue working at the program.

This philosophy, which is the basis of relapse prevention, is essential. You must never let a slip or a lapse sabotage you in returning to your habits. Everyone makes mistakes. Those who learn from their mistakes are more likely to succeed. Those who put too much energy into beating themselves up over the slip, or use it as an excuse to go back to old habits, will limit their chances at success. Adhere to this philosophy, today, this week, and forever. Do not, however, use this as permission to have a slip.

If you had a slip, it is important to analyze the events and feelings that were present during that day. Take the time to reflect upon and write down your answers to the following questions about the event that led to the slip:

1. What happened this week that led me to smoke additional cigarettes?

2. How was I feeling at the time?

3. Was this a typical event or feeling, or was it unexpected and took me by surprise?

4. What could I have said to myself (self-talk) to dissuade me from smoking?

5. What could I have done in this situation instead of smoking?

6. What have I learned from this situation?

Whether you had a slip, or were compliant with the limit, renew your commitment to quit smoking and give yourself that much deserved pat on the back for continuing with the program. By taking one day at a time, you can feel even more confident in your ability to become and remain a nonsmoker.

Hypnosis

Last week you learned how to achieve a deep state of relaxation though a procedure known as Progressive Muscle Relaxation. Relaxation is a very effective stress management technique. If you were successful with the procedure, you may have noticed yourself becoming tremendously relaxed, where you were able to block out distractions, and feel completely at peace. Almost like a twilight sleep. This state is what is referred to as a trance. A trance state is a natural state where our unconscious mind is able to process information, while our conscious mind is distracted by being highly focused on another stimulus. At one time or another you may have been so preoccupied with a thought that you drove right past your exit; that same exit that you take day after day. Or perhaps you've caught yourself daydreaming in a staff meeting, while your head is nodding in chorus with your colleagues, as if you've heard every word the boss has said. These are trance states. Your mind becomes so intensely focused that you are not consciously aware of what you are doing. Somehow you arrived safely at your destination, and didn't get demoted for not paying attention at the meeting. Your unconscious mind had taken over.

How then, does hypnosis work? Hypnosis allows you to access your unconscious mind by distracting your conscious mind. This is done by focusing on an object or on certain images, until the unconscious mind becomes more accessible. Then, instructions or metaphors are introduced to the unconscious mind. For smoking, thoughts or images about the undesirability of the taste of cigarettes may be introduced. The connections between certain activities and smoking may be broken, or messages about your inner strengths and abilities to be a nonsmoker may be given.

It is important to remember that you are always in control during all phases of hypnosis, and that nobody can ever make you do anything you wouldn't want to do. So unless you have a lifelong desire to cluck like a chicken, nobody can force that foul behavior upon you. Hypnosis is very safe, with no side effects, unless you have a problem with psychosis or have feelings of dissociation (where you feel that you are outside of your body at times). If you suspect that you have these problems, stay away from hypnosis, and consider being evaluated by a reputable psychologist or psychiatrist.

Hypnosis alone has been shown to have a success rate of 50% for smoking cessation for a period of up to 6 months. Combining it with a structured smoking program, such as Quit for Life and good support increase the success rate significantly.

Hypnosis can be done individually with a trained hypnotherapist, in small or large groups, or through pre-taped audio tapes. A good hypnotherapist will also provide you with a hypnosis tape to use at home for daily practice. The more often you utilize the hypnosis, the more confident you will be, increasing your likelihood of success.

The cost of smoking cessation hypnosis varies considerably. The least expensive in-person hypnosis sessions are done in a large group format (approximately 200 people). The average cost is around $40. They also give you the option of buying an audio tape for home practice for $20 or more. We highly recommend that if you attend a session that you buy the tape. This brings the total to approximately $60.

Individual sessions usually cost between $110 and $150, and usually include an audio tape of your session.

Hypnosis tapes can also be purchased through self-improvement catalogs. They typically range in price from $16 - $50 plus shipping and handling. As mentioned last week, a tape can be also be purchased through our web site: www.InterPersonalNet.com for $11.95 + $3.95 shipping and handling ($15.90 total plus tax). It contains both the Progressive Muscle Relaxation and Smoking Cessation Hypnosis inductions. No matter which technique you pick, if any, use the tape on a regular basis, even for a few weeks after you quit. It will improve your long term success.

Quit Today!

Today is the big day! Last week you signed the Stop Smoking Contract. You have made a commitment to yourself to stop smoking. To rid yourself of any temptation, you must do the following:

1. Throw away all of your cigarettes.

2. Dispose of your lighters and ashtrays.

3. Dispose of, or make inaccessible, any other paraphernalia that you closely associate with smoking. Do the same at your workplace.

4. Make a verbal proclamation in front of others that you have finally quit!

Many people feel more gratification from undertaking these actions in a small ceremony. For example, if one of your reasons for quitting is for the benefit of your family, include your spouse and children in the honors, as you demonstrate your commitment to them and to the process. Allow the children to each throw a lighter or ashtray into the garbage, and help you carry them to the curb. Follow this up with a small celebration (e.g., an "I Quit" cake or a trip to the ice cream parlor or movies).

Over the course of the next week, you will likely feel a variety of feelings about your decision to quit. Some people feel invigorated, proud, and strong, while others feel fear of failure, self-doubt or depressed feelings. You may alternate between positive and negative feelings. If you begin to feel any negative feelings or self-doubt, examine these feelings. Remind yourself that you are experiencing them because you have made a decision to make a significant positive change in your life. Reframe these feelings as a side-effect of smoking cessation. They cannot be allowed to undermine your success. Like minor side-effects of medications, they can be tolerated if you focus on the benefit.

Some Handy Tips:

- Get your teeth cleaned and whitened.

- Get the interior of your car cleaned and deodorized.

- Do not allow others to smoke in your house or car (providing your spouse or roommate doesn't smoke. If they do smoke, ask them to be supportive by smoking in a specific area, or only in their car, for at least the next month).

- Remind your supportive others what you need from them (encouragement, keeping you occupied, or not mentioning your quitting) to bolster your success.

- Make a simultaneous commitment to eat better and to exercise, to make your overall lifestyle more healthy.

- Keep your hands occupied. Learn to crochet or knit.

- Keep gum or candy with you at all times.

- Munch on healthy foods such as carrot and celery sticks or popcorn when you feel you need to have something in your mouth.

- Cut a straw in half (to about the length of a cigarette), put it in your mouth and take a few deep breaths through it.

- Continuously praise yourself with self-talk for a job well done.

- Remember to use deep breathing frequently during the day.

Understanding How Your Body is Already Repairing Itself: Withdrawal Effects

Dependency on cigarettes is twofold: behavioral and physical. For many individuals breaking the physical dependency, or addiction, to nicotine is of equal difficulty. On the positive side, the withdrawal symptoms don't last very long, and diminish in intensity day by day.

Withdrawal symptoms vary from person to person. Some individuals feel no symptoms, while others report significant physical and emotional symptoms. One factor that influences the strength of the withdrawal effects is the amount of nicotine in your system. Since you have been cutting down on your nicotine intake for three weeks, you should feel a minimal amount of withdrawal effects.

It takes approximately seven days to completely eliminate nicotine from your body. The majority of the nicotine is eliminated in the first three or four days. Withdrawal effects will be the strongest during this time. Nicotine is eliminated from the body through the kidneys. For this reason, it is suggested that you increase your intake of water and clear juices.

The most common withdrawal symptoms of nicotine include:

- coughing

- dizziness/lightheadedness

- nervousness

- shakiness

- headaches

- irritability

- difficulty concentrating

- shortness of breath

- sweating

- disrupted sleep

- heart palpitations

- feeling lethargic

You may feel some, all, or none of these withdrawal symptoms in the next week. Theses feelings may be difficult to ignore. Because the discomfort of withdrawal can be temporarily terminated by smoking a single cigarette, you may feel tempted to stop your suffering by slipping back into old habits. These temptations can be reduced or eliminated by viewing these feelings in a positive way through a technique called positive reframing.

Positive reframing is a method of viewing a problem from a positive perspective. For smoking cessation, it is a way of viewing the negative side effects of quitting as the positive symptoms of your body recovering. Your body is healing itself from the effects of the years of nicotine and toxins. You must learn how to reinterpret these withdrawal symptoms as recovery symptoms.

The majority of these symptoms are elicited through either the nervous system or as the result of improved respiratory system response. For instance, feelings of lightheadedness is the result of increased oxygen to the brain. Your lungs begin to repair themselves immediately, allowing for more intake of oxygen. In addition, the carbon monoxide in cigarette smoke decreases the amount of oxygen in your blood. When you stop smoking, your blood carries up to 15% more oxygen throughout your body. Within 12 hours, the oxygen level in the blood increases. This can result in feelings of lightheadedness or dizziness, as your brain is not accustomed to receiving this much oxygen.

If you begin to feel dizzy, don't feel defeated by viewing it as another means of self-inflicted discomfort. Instead, view it for what it is: You're body's way of recovering. Say to yourself "I feel dizzy and lightheaded because my brain is receiving more oxygen."

Coughing is the lungs' process of clearing themselves of the tar and carcinogens. The cilia, or hair-like cells that line the lungs are regenerating and beginning to function better. Coughing allows the cilia to eliminate the carcinogens from your lungs, resulting in increased coughing and mucous. You will tolerate these recovery symptoms better by viewing them as the body's means of repairing itself, rather than as a negative symptom. They will go away with time. Although this technique may sound foolish, it is extremely helpful in increasing your tolerance to your body's recovery symptoms.

Remember to also reframe the emotional symptoms you may be experiencing as the result of nicotine withdrawal. Each symptom you experience should be viewed as your body's reaction to return to a drug-free state. For instance, if you are feeling agitated or short-tempered, remind yourself that it is a temporary sign of breaking the addiction to nicotine, and that your nervous system is beginning to function properly, without the drug. Be sure to use positive self-talk such as "this will only last for a few days" or "I am a strong person, I know I'll make it through." This will also help you to cope and tolerate the recovery effects.

Over the next 24 hours list the most common withdrawal symptoms you experience: In the right hand column, write down your re-conceptualization of these symptoms, followed by thoughts that can help you to more easily tolerate them.

For example:

Symptom	Reason (Reconceptualization)
Irritability	1. *My nervous system is beginning to function normally without stimulants* 2. *This should only last a few days. I'll be able to cope even better in the near future with all of the new coping skills I've learned.*

88

Withdrawal Symptoms

Symptom	Reason (Reconceptualization)

Fighting Cravings and Urges

As we discussed, the physical cravings for nicotine should diminish by the end of this week. The psychological cravings, however, can last a lifetime. On the positive side, they too diminish in intensity and frequency with time. Its like feeding a stray dog. If you set food out on your back stoop for a stray, he will continue to show up. More frequently at first, and less frequently with time, if food is not provided. The less you feed him, the less often he will come looking for scraps. Eventually, he will stop coming around. If after three weeks of not feeding him, you feel badly, and give him scraps "just this once" you can be certain that he will be coming around tomorrow, and the next day, and the day after that.

Giving in to urges and cravings is the same as giving food to the stray. The less you reinforce that craving, the less it will come around. If you think that you can give in to it just this once, you begin the entire cycle of cravings and urges all over again. Skinner and his rats demonstrated that a learned behavior which was previously extinguished will return *after only one reinforcement!* It then becomes *more difficult* to extinguish than before.

Like any physical or emotional sensation, the first step is always identification of the sensation. In the past, you automatically responded to cravings or urges, by giving it what it wanted: a cigarette. The urge went away, and you didn't think twice. You can no longer respond in that same manner. You have to be aware of what the sensation of the craving is like, identify it for what it is, and find another way to get rid of it.

The following is a list of ways to respond to physical and/or psychological cravings:

- Use self-talk to remind you that the withdrawal symptoms are only temporary.

- Reframe your symptoms in terms of how they are signs that your body is already repairing itself.

- Munch on healthy foods such as carrot and celery sticks or popcorn when you feel you need to have something in your mouth.

- Drink a lot of water and clear juices. This helps your body clear itself of toxins.

- Watch your caffeine intake. Since nicotine acts on the metabolism, you may not be able to tolerate as much caffeine once you stop smoking. This can result in similar symptoms as nicotine withdrawal (e.g., irritability and nervousness).

- Increase your physical activity. If you feel a craving, go for a brisk walk or exercise (in a manner medically approved for you). This will stimulate the endorphins, your body's natural stimulants, and make you feel healthier. It will also facilitate the healing of the lungs through clearing out the toxic substances.

- Go to a place where smoking is not allowed, such as the shopping mall, the movies, the library or bookstore.

- If you are a spiritual individual, pray for strength and guidance.

- Distract yourself by engaging in an activity which is typically not linked to smoking. Avoid those that are linked with smoking, such as talking on the phone, etc.

- Do something that is healthy or self-nurturing, such as taking a hot bath or giving yourself a facial.

- Talk to someone about your cravings, and ask them for their assistance in distracting you or talking you through them.

- Use deep breathing. It increases the amount of oxygen to the brain and is very calming.

- Review your list of reasons for quitting (Week One).

Identifying Alternative Pleasurable Activities

This will likely be the most difficult week for you in the quitting process. Some people feel a great sense of loss, or feel depressed or blue when they give up their long-term relationship with cigarettes. Therefore, it is important to plan an extra pleasurable activity for each day in this week, to help replace this sense of loss. It doesn't need to be a large scale activity, or a big demand on your time. It is important to keep the activity reasonable for your lifestyle. It could be something as small as taking a hot relaxing bubble bath, giving yourself 30 minutes of undisturbed time to read your favorite novel, seeing a movie, or doing deep muscle relaxation. This is much like the rewards that you established in week 2, but these are specific activities with which you will reward yourself and pamper yourself.

Write down the chosen activity for each day of the week, starting with today, preferably immediately following your quitting ceremony. It is advisable that you transfer these plans to your calendar or PDA.

Day of the Week   **Planned Activity**

1.

2.

3.

4.

5.

6.

7.

Although not required, it is recommended that you continue to plan these activities over the course of the next few weeks. If you feel that you don't have time to reward yourself in small ways, or that it is difficult to give yourself permission to pamper yourself take a few minutes to examine these thoughts. Whether it is self-esteem, or feeling guilty about taking valuable time away from your family, you may have just identified some of the underlying reasons that have led to past failures.

Avoiding Weight Gain

On average, people gain between four and seven pounds when they stop smoking. Some individuals will gain no weight, while others may put on more than 7 pounds. This is mostly contingent upon what you eat and how active you are.

There are several reasons why people tend to gain weight when they quit smoking. Some are the result of biological changes in the body, including a decrease in metabolic rate and improved sense of taste and smell, and others are the result of behaviors and habits, such as feeling the need to have something in your mouth. Whatever the reason, it is important to stay on top of your weight if this is a concern for you.

Nicotine, like most stimulants, raises the body's metabolic rate. The higher the metabolic rate, the faster the body burns up energy. When you eliminate nicotine, the body's metabolic rate decreases. Therefore, you are not burning as many calories as you were when smoking. In addition, nicotine tends to act as an appetite suppressor. So now you may feel hungry more often. Don't allow this to be an excuse for returning to smoking. Instead, make sure that you are using appropriate substitute behaviors that will not add to your weight. Some suggestions are included later in this section. Another reason that weight gain is typical with smoking cessation is that your sense of smell and taste are returning to normal. You may have noticed that your senses of smell and taste are heightened since you stopped smoking. Many people begin to enjoy the flavor of food more, and as a result, tend to overindulge. Allow yourself to enjoy the aromas and flavors of food, but don't get carried away.

Probably the most common reason for weight gain after quitting smoking is behavioral. It is not uncommon to begin to snack more often, mostly as a substitute for the hand-mouth action that has been a habit since your first cigarette. Sometimes it is nothing more than the result of frustration of not having anything to do with your hands or your mouth. If this is your downfall, make sure to substitute low-calorie snacks that will satisfy that need for hand-mouth action. While gum or candy can help by keeping your mouth occupied, you may also need to find something to keep your hands busy.

In Week Two, we discussed the tendency of some individuals to feel that they are denying themselves by not smoking. Some try to make up for this deprivation by nurturing themselves with food. This is OK, providing you do not go overboard. It is preferable for you to gain five or ten pounds than to return to smoking. For the average person, it is much healthier to gain a few pounds than to smoke. To have the same negative health risks as smoking one pack of cigarettes per day, you would need to gain at least 65 pounds. In fact, mortality rates associated with being overweight approach the mortality associated with smoking only when weight exceeds 110% of normal body weight (Van Itallie, 1992). You can always focus on losing the weight later.

Be careful not to gain too much weight, as this will likely result in decreased self-esteem, which can sabotage your success. If you do gain weight, remember to utilize self-talk to reinforce your progress, rather than to beat yourself up for eating more. Remind yourself that you are taking action to improve your lifestyle and your health. Whether or not weight gain is an issue, make exercise a priority. It is an excellent stress reliever, which can help to alleviate some of the tension that you may be experiencing. It will also activate some of your endorphins, those "happy" chemicals in your body, which are more natural substitute for the stimulation that your body has been receiving from nicotine. It will also help you feel that you are able to effect change (self-efficacy) by improving your lifestyle, and becoming healthier.

Exercise can be one of the best responses to a craving. After a brisk walk, or a 5 minute ride on an exercise bike, your craving will likely pass. When possible, begin to exercise as soon as a craving begins. It will not only distract you from the craving, but increase your feelings of self-efficacy. It will also increase your oxygen consumption that can help speed up your lungs' recovery.

The most important thing you can do is focus on your success with quitting smoking. The best approach is to initiate an overall change of lifestyle into a healthier one. If you view this as a lifestyle change, you will be less likely to feel deprived, and will feel more empowered. Begin to utilize better coping skills, in addition to eating better, beginning to exercise, and stopping your smoking.

Caution yourself against eating more in response to stress. In the past, you grabbed a cigarette and began to smoke in response to stress. Utilize your new coping skills, such as relaxation, self-talk, distraction, or exercise to cope with stress, rather than reacting to it by eating. Excess eating is simply a substitution of one inappropriate coping response for another.

Avoiding Weight Gain: Some More Tips

- Drink a minimum of eight glasses of water, as well as clear juices. This will help you feel satiated, while helping your system flush out toxins.

- Avoid desserts after meals. This will not only help with weight management, but can help you to avoid cravings from the coffee-dessert-cigarette triad.

- Substitute with low calorie foods, such as unbuttered popcorn, fresh fruits and vegetables.

- Keep sugarless gum and/or candy available to fight cravings.

- Keep celery and carrot sticks already cut up and available in the refrigerator.

- Begin an exercise program. Get your quitting buddy or significant other involved to help keep you motivated.

- Increase your daily activity level by using the stairs instead of the elevator, or parking your car in the back of the parking lot and walking further to the door of the office or store.

- Go for a short walk, or do a few sit-ups when you feel the urge to smoke.

- Engage in short bouts of exercise several times a day to energize you.

- Begin to view yourself as healthier, rather than focusing on your weight.

Remember that this week will be the most challenging of them all. Keep your motivation going and give your smoking cessation efforts all of the energy and attention they deserve. Keep this book close at hand, as well as your list of reasons for quitting to redirect yourself if you are feeling any urges or temptations.

Week Five: Relapse Prevention

- Relapse Prevention: Remaining a Nonsmoker

- Identifying High Risk Situations

- Setbacks and Slips

- Combating Rationalizations

- Reward Yourself

Welcome to Week 5 of the Quit for Life smoking cessation program. This is a very exciting, but potentially frightening week for most individuals. By now, the majority of your recovery symptoms have passed. The worst is over, but there is still work to be done if you wish to remain a nonsmoker forever.

If you have been successful in not smoking at all for the past week: Congratulations! If you've had a difficult time stopping, or have had a slip or two, don't give up. You've come too far to go back to old habits. If you had more than four slips in the past week, go back and repeat Week 4 from the beginning. Return to Week 5 next week after successfully completing a full week of not smoking.

The focus of this week is to help you remain a nonsmoker. We will focus on the situations that place you at highest risk for relapse (slipping back) and teach you how to best cope with, or avoid, those situations. This is a critical factor that deserves great attention. You have probably been successful at quitting a number of times in the past, but were unable to *remain* a nonsmoker. That may be the result of most programs' failure to address the means of remaining a nonsmoker. Successful prevention of relapses is what allows today's ex-smokers to remain ex-smokers forever.

Relapse Prevention: Remaining a Nonsmoker

In previous chapters you have been asked to look over the prior week to identify "slips" or "lapses" when you had an unpermitted cigarette. You were asked to evaluate the circumstances surrounding your decision to smoke and learn from it. This is the basis of relapse prevention.

As a human being, an occasional slip or lapse into old habits is not unusual. They will likely occur, but they should not invalidate your progress and set you back to day one. For example: After a hard day, you and your spouse get into an argument and you storm out of the house.   Out of anger, frustration and hurt, you reach for a cigarette and have a smoke. This is referred to as a *lapse, setback* or *slip*. It is a momentary slip back into old patterns. At this point, you need to make a decision: Do I get back on the program? or do I beat myself up and sabotage myself by giving up completely and returning to the old smoking habits? The latter situation where there is complete failure and a return to where you started is referred to as a *relapse*.

By throwing up your hands and giving up ("I'm never going to be successful anyway, so I might as well give up") you return to becoming a full smoker. For many individuals, a relapse results in smoking even more cigarettes than you had typically smoked in the past. It also lowers your confidence level and threatens self-esteem. This makes it even more difficult to successfully quit in the future.

Effective prevention of relapses is twofold: learning how to prevent slips from occurring; and learning how to respond to setbacks and slips to avoid having them become full blown relapses. The next two sections will address both of these steps to assure your success as a nonsmoker.

Identifying High Risk Situations:

The first step in preventing slips from occurring is to identify "high risk situations." These are the situations or feelings that put you at higher risk for smoking. The people, places, situations, and emotions that were associated with the "most needed cigarettes" on your Daily Self-Monitoring Sheets are likely to be your high risk situations. You may wish to look over Week Two's "Review of Self-Monitoring Sheets" to assist you in identifying your high risk situations. They could be a specific setting (e.g., a bar or night club), certain people (e.g., old smoking buddies or an irritating relative), or specific feelings (e.g., stress, anger, or depression). By identifying your high risk situations, you can develop contingency plans for coping, thereby reducing, or even eliminating, your risk for a lapse or relapse.

The following exercise will help you to identify your specific high risk situations as well as coping skills and appropriate responses to these specific situations. The purpose is to develop a plan of action and to mentally rehearse these strategies, helping you to avoid or to cope with these inevitable situations. Try to avoid these high risk situations until you are a well established nonsmoker. If you cannot avoid them, you need to identify ways of coping with the situations to avoid a lapse. Complete the left hand column by identifying those situations that are likely to be the riskiest for you. In the right hand column, write down an action plan that you could use to avoid this situation altogether. Also identify one or more positive coping responses that you can use to avoid the situation. If you are having difficulty completing the right hand column, return to week 3 to review the various coping strategies.

Example:

High Risk Situations	Planned Action (Coping Response)
Break room at work	1. Take breaks elsewhere 2. Go for a walk on my break 3. Bring a book to read and gum to chew during break
Feeling tense	1. Use my relaxation tape 2. Use self-talk to calm me down 3. Remind myself how well I've done so far, don't want to slip back into smoking 4. Exercise/Go for a walk

Coping with High Risk Situations

In the first column of this table list any high risk situations which might trigger you to slip back into old habits. In the second column list actions (coping responses) you can take to prevent those situations from causing a permanent relapse.

High Risk Situations	Planned Action (Coping Response)

Setbacks and Slips

The second step to relapse prevention is knowing how to respond to a setback or slip to prevent it from becoming a relapse. This is where self-talk can be an invaluable tool. The key is to learn from the slip, and continue moving in a positive direction.

In our work with weight management, we cannot tell you how many times clients have allowed one mistake to sabotage their whole diet. One ice cream sundae has led them to throw up their hands, feel like a failure, and punish themselves by eating a whole bag of cookies. They made sure, however, to take a three second break between inhaling each Oreo™, to tell themselves that "I am such a loser" and that "I can never do anything right." This negative self-talk allowed them to sabotage their whole diet. They gained back the fifteen pounds they lost, with an extra bonus of five pounds for being such a failure. This was before they learned about relapse prevention. They now know how to overlook a temporary slip and learn from it, allowing themselves to continue their success.

A setback may be inevitable. It should be viewed as an opportunity to learn from the situation, so you can avoid a lapse in the future. Make a few copies of this next exercise to keep with you over the next few weeks. Should you have a setback, complete the form immediately. This will help you learn the appropriate ways to respond to slips. It will also help you to focus and to direct you back onto the correct path.

Learning from Setbacks and Slips

1. What happened that led me to smoke after I worked so hard to quit?

    _____

2. What was I feeling at the time?

    _____

3. Was this a typical feeling or event, or was it unexpected and took me by surprise?

    _____

4. What could I have said to myself (self-talk) to dissuade me from smoking?

    _____

5. What could I have done in this situation instead of smoking?

    _____

6. What have I learned from this situation?

    _____

7. How will I handle this, or a similar situation, in the future?

    _____

Combating Rationalizations

On some occasions, individuals consciously choose to smoke a cigarette, even after several weeks of successful abstinence. They justify it to themselves through rationalizations. This is the means by which we give ourselves a rationale for what we did, or what we are about to do. For example: "This was an awful day at work, I'm going to have a cigarette to calm myself down" or "I really did a good job on that project. I'm going to treat myself to a cigarette." Another very common and dangerous rationalization is: "I'll only have one. Tomorrow I will get back on the program."

This negative self-talk is just another way of playing "head games" with yourself. It is appropriate to use positive self-talk to convince yourself NOT to smoke, or to recover from a setback. It is not appropriate to use this type of self-talk to rationalize having a cigarette, especially making this rationalization **before** you smoke.

Common rationalizations include:

- Using cigarettes as a reward for a job well done: "I deserve a treat."

- Allowing yourself to smoke because a situation was stressful or uncomfortable "I need a cigarette to relax."

- Telling yourself that "one won't hurt" or "I'll go back on the program after this one."

Think back to previous smoking cessation attempts, where you were successful in quitting, but relapsed back into old habits. What type of rationalizations did you use? How many times have you told yourself that one cigarette will not make a difference?

Be aware if you begin to use rationalizations. The minute these justifications come into your head, a warning alarm should sound. You must combat these through the use of realistic challenges, and then substitute them with positive self-talk. If you are unsure whether it is a rationalization, ask yourself this: What would my supportive/significant other say about this statement? Would (s)he find this believable or feel that I am just playing mind games? You can also ask someone who has successfully quit, or someone in a smoking cessation chat room whether or not it is a rationalization. Remember, if your actions are appropriate, you should not feel the need to rationalize. If you do rationalize, your actions are likely inappropriate. Otherwise, why would you be rationalizing?

Rationalization	Challenge to Rationalization	Substitute for Rationalization
Allowing myself to smoke because a situation was stressful "I need a cigarette to relax."	Nicotine is a stimulant; it will only add to my tension	I'll go for a short walk to help me relax.

Rationalization Exercise

In the first column of this table list any rationalizations which you might use as an excuse to slip back into old habits. In the second column list a challenge to each rationalization. In the third column write a substitute for the rationalization which you can use instead.

Rationalization	Challenge to Rationalization	Substitute for Rationalization

Reward Yourself

It is essential that you continue to reward yourself for a very difficult week. Review your list of rewards for this week that you identified in Week Two. Be sure to include a lot of self-praise. Remember to use self-talk to combat any feelings of deprivation from not smoking. Continue to view withdrawal symptoms as recovery symptoms, and allow yourself to experience them as a positive sensation rather than a negative one. You should also continue with the relaxation or hypnosis on a daily basis for at least the next two weeks.

Indulge in self-gratification. You've worked very hard!

Week Six: Remaining a Nonsmoker for Life

- Reviewing your Success

- Assessing New Coping Skills

- Anticipating High Risk Situations

- Remaining a Nonsmoker for Life!

You have reached the final week of the Quit for Life smoking cessation program. The worst is behind you! While it becomes progressively easier to remain a nonsmoker with time, you cannot stop working at it yet. This is the point where most people relapse. The pride and enthusiasm of quitting begins to diminish, making it easier to fall back into old patterns. You may feel overly confident and fail to put energy into continuing your progress. Almost every smoker has been able to quit at one time or another. Remaining a nonsmoker is where you've likely had difficulty before. This time, you can make it a permanent change!

Reviewing your Success

It is time to once again review your progress to date. If you were unable to abstain from smoking, or had a serious relapse, with more than five slips in the past week, you need to return to Week Four now. Don't fool yourself into pushing through this week if you were not able to successfully complete Week Four or Five. This is not a race, and you will obtain "nonsmoker" status at the time you successfully and permanently quit.

If you have been successful, we wish to congratulate you for a job well done! By now, nearly all of your recovery symptoms have faded. The physical cravings and urges should have also decreased. Most of the challenges that you will face in the upcoming weeks are the psychological or habitual factors associated with smoking. You will need to actively face these challenges for the next few weeks, until you no longer feel a strong temptation to return to cigarettes. You need to integrate the coping skills that you have learned, in order to make lifelong changes.

Assess your current coping skills to see which of your old skills you have improved and to see which new skills you have adopted. Next identify your high risk situations for the next two weeks, and review the tips provided in chapter four to make you a nonsmoker for life.

Assessing New Coping Skills

The past six weeks may have been some of the most stressful times that you have experienced in the recent past. This may be in part because you felt that you were robbed of one of your most familiar and comforting coping techniques. You may have surprised yourself that you could actually survive conflict, tension and frustration without a cigarette! We knew you could!

To better cope with stress, you need to be aware of your reactions to stress. Think about a stressful situation you have faced in the past week. How did you respond to this situation? What are the physical responses you may have had in response to this situation?

As you are aware, there are numerous coping skills available. As creatures of habit, we tend to utilize the same few techniques whenever we are faced with stress. We often feel comfortable with the skills we have used repeatedly in the past. In Chapter Three we discussed the importance of stress management and introduced a variety of coping techniques. Take a moment to assess the coping tools you have used. Some of them you have used prior to beginning this program. Hopefully you have learned other techniques through this program.

Check off the coping tools or techniques with which you have been successful :

☐ Talk to others/use support   ☐ Distract myself/keep busy

☐ Pray   ☐ Think about possible solutions

☐ Use relaxation or meditation   ☐ Look for the silver lining

☐ Talk to myself (self-talk)   ☐ Exercise/physically release tension

☐ Seek more information   ☐ Be assertive

☐ Make a list of available   ☐ Ask others how they would handle the

   options   situation

☐ Listen to music   ☐ Tell myself "things could be worse"

☐ Use deep breathing   ☐ Try to understand the other's point of

                                         view

☐ Other techniques I used:

_____

☐ Coping techniques that I wish to improve or add to my repertoire are:

_____

If some of these skills are not already part of your coping repertoire, they should be learned and integrated into your current set of skills. These techniques will not only be helpful for conquering smoking, but are essential in effectively dealing with any type of stress. We encourage you to continue to develop and improve your coping skills. This will allow you to be more effective and also contribute to a sense of confidence and self-esteem.

Anticipating High Risk situations

Last week, you learned about high risk situations, and worked on identifying and anticipating them. By identifying your high risk situations, you will develop contingency plans for coping, thereby reducing, or even eliminating, your risk for a lapse or relapse.

The following exercise will help you to identify your specific high risk situations as well as coping skills and appropriate responses to these specific situations. The purpose is to develop a plan of action and to mentally rehearse these strategies, helping you to avoid or to cope with these inevitable situations.

Think ahead for the next two weeks. Identify those situations that you feel are going to be "high risk." As you did last week, write down the high risk situations that you anticipate for the next two weeks in the left hand column. In the right hand column, write down one or more positive coping responses or plans that you could use to avoid this situation altogether.

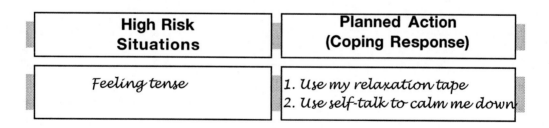

High Risk Situations	Planned Action (Coping Response)
Feeling tense	1. Use my relaxation tape 2. Use self-talk to calm me down

Coping with High Risk Situations

In the first column of this table list any high risk situations which might trigger you to slip back into old habits. In the second column list actions (coping responses) you can take to prevent those situations from causing a permanent relapse.

High Risk Situations	Planned Action (Coping Response)

Remaining a Nonsmoker for Life!

You have just completed one of the most comprehensive smoking cessation programs available. Whether you weaned down or you used a nicotine substitute, you've worked hard to become a nonsmoker. You owe it to yourself and your friends and family to continue working at remaining a nonsmoker. We have given you the tools and the ability to remain a nonsmoker for life. You must keep up the motivation, especially over the next few weeks.

The following tips will assist you in maintaining your progress so you can enjoy being a nonsmoker for life!

- Remember that a setback may be inevitable. It should be used as an opportunity to learn from the situation, so you can avoid a lapse in the future.

- Use a smoking cessation chat room to continue to gain support. You may also wish to be a source of encouragement to your fellow quitters through a difficult process.

- Continue to reward yourself. Follow through with the rewards that you established in week 2. This includes rewards for this week, as well as monthly rewards for the next 6 months.

- Circle the anniversary of your quit date on your calendar for a big reward. Calculate the amount of money you saved from not smoking for one year, and consider using it for a vacation, or to buy something special for yourself.

- Continue to praise yourself for a job well done. You know how hard you worked. This will also reinforce your confidence which is necessary to remain a nonsmoker for life.

- Never let your guard down. Although your your cravings and urges will diminish with time, you must be proactive in your goal to remain smoke-free. You've worked too hard to return to smoking.

- Continue to use the skills that you have learned to cope with stress and unexpected situations in the future.

- If you have a hypnosis tape, continue to use it. This will fortify your success in abstaining, and will make you more resistant to urges and cravings.

- *Never* fool yourself by thinking that you can have only one cigarette, no matter how long you've been a nonsmoker. We continue to hear horror stories of people that think that they are immune to relapse, and return to their old habits after five or ten years. We are not telling you that you will have to stay actively involved in abstaining from smoking forever, but being completely passive will likely lead to a relapse.

We hope that this has been a positive and useful experience for you. We wish you continue success in remaining a nonsmoker, and also for continuing with a more healthy lifestyle. Remember, if you should have any slips, or feel increased urges, refer back to the appropriate sections of the book to help you refocus on ways to achieve your goal. Keep your confidence and motivation going!

Appendix: Forms to Photocopy & Use

- Cigarette Monitoring Form (front)

- Cigarette Monitoring Form (back)

- No Smoking Contract

The Cigarette Monitoring Forms are meant to be copied to both sides of a brightly colored piece of paper, then cut into quarters to make four forms which can be slipped into the plastic sleeve of your cigarette packs. You will need to make enough of these for three weeks of monitoring. If you do not have a photocopier, any copy center or "quick printer" can make the copies for you. If you have a computer and printer you may download PDF (Portable Document Format) versions of these forms and print them out yourself. The PDFs may be downloaded from our web site:

http://interpersonalnet.com/quitforlife/

The No Smoking Contract may be used either within this book, or you may choose to have it photocopied onto parchment paper or some other paper suitable for framing.

Quit for Life Cigarette Monitoring Form

Day/Date: _____ Week #: _____

#	Time	Need 1 (least) -10	Activity or Place	With Whom?	Mood or Reason
1					
2					
3					
4					
5					
6					
7					
8					
9					
10					

Quit for Life Cigarette Monitoring Form

Day/Date: _____ Week #: _____

#	Time	Need 1 (least) -10	Activity or Place	With Whom?	Mood or Reason
1					
2					
3					
4					
5					
6					
7					
8					
9					
10					

Quit for Life Cigarette Monitoring Form

Day/Date: _____ Week #: _____

#	Time	Need 1 (least) -10	Activity or Place	With Whom?	Mood or Reason
1					
2					
3					
4					
5					
6					
7					
8					
9					
10					

Quit for Life Cigarette Monitoring Form

Day/Date: _____ Week #: _____

#	Time	Need 1 (least) -10	Activity or Place	With Whom?	Mood or Reason
1					
2					
3					
4					
5					
6					
7					
8					
9					
10					

Quit for Life Cigarette Monitoring Form

Day/Date: _____ Week #: _____

#	Time	Need 1 (least) -10	Activity or Place	With Whom?	Mood or Reason
11					
12					
13					
14					
15					
16					
17					
18					
19					
20					

Quit for Life Cigarette Monitoring Form

Day/Date: _____ Week #: _____

#	Time	Need 1 (least) -10	Activity or Place	With Whom?	Mood or Reason
11					
12					
13					
14					
15					
16					
17					
18					
19					
20					

Quit for Life Cigarette Monitoring Form

Day/Date: _____ Week #: _____

#	Time	Need 1 (least) -10	Activity or Place	With Whom?	Mood or Reason
11					
12					
13					
14					
15					
16					
17					
18					
19					
20					

Quit for Life Cigarette Monitoring Form

Day/Date: _____ Week #: _____

#	Time	Need 1 (least) -10	Activity or Place	With Whom?	Mood or Reason
11					
12					
13					
14					
15					
16					
17					
18					
19					
20					

QUIT FOR LIFE NO SMOKING CONTRACT

I, _____ (*your name*), hereby affirm that I am motivated and committed to quit smoking. Some of the reasons which compel me to quit and support my commitment are:

I have decided that smoking is no longer acceptable for me. Therefore I am making a promise to myself and my family that I will not smoke after my quit date of _____. If I find myself tempted to smoke, I promise to call _____ for support.

_____
Signed

_____
Witness

_____
Date

References

American Cancer Society (2002). Quitting smoking adds years to tour life, regardless of age. *CA Cancer Journal for Clinicians.* American Cancer Society, *52*; 319.

American Cancer Society (2002;1996;1982). *Cancer Facts and Figures.* American Cancer Society, Atlanta GA.

American Lung Association *(2003). Trends in Tobacco Use.* American Lung Association Epidemiology and Statistics Unit, Research and Scientific Affairs.

Arizona Smokers Helpline (2003). http://.ashline.org

Hyder Ferry, L. (1999). Non-nicotine pharmacotherapy for smoking cessation. *Primary Care: Clinics in Office Practice, 26(3),* 653-669.

Jorenby, D.E. (1999). A controlled trial of sustained release bupropion, a nicotine patch, or both for smoking cessation. *New England Journal of Medicine, 340(9),* 685-691.

Glaxowellcome (2003). http://Zyban.com.

Taylor, D. H., Hasselblad, V., Henley, S.J., Thun, M. J., & Sloan, F.A. (2002). Benefits of smoking cessation for longevity. *American Journal of Public Health. 92,* 990-996.

U.S. Department of Health and Human Services (1990). *The Health Benefits of Smoking Cessation. A Report of the Surgeon General.* U.S. Department of Health and Human Services, Public Health Service, Office on Smoking and Health.

VanItallie, T. B. (1992). Body weight, morbidity, and longevity. In P. Bjorntrop & B. N. Brodoff (Eds.), *Obesity.* Philadelphia: Lippincott. 361-369.

Quit for Life
Quick Order Form

To Place an Order:
Call (585) 889-7627 or
FAX your Order Form to (585) 271-7313 or
Via web at http://interpersonalnet.com
Mail your order to: Dr. Kathryn Vullo
4 Chelmsford Road
Rochester, New York 14618

Item	Price	Qty	Total
Quit for Life: A Clinical Guide to Smoking Cessation	$16.95		
Relaxation Training & Hypnosis Audio Tape	$11.95		
Book & Tape Together	$24.95		

Product Total: $ _____

New York Residents add 8.25% Sales Tax: $ _____

Shipping (see chart below): $ _____

Grand Total: $ _____

Shipping

Within the U.S.	Outside the U.S.
$5 for the first book	$9 for the first book
$3 for each additional book.	$4 for each additional book.
$4 for each cassette tape	$6 for each cassette tape
$7 for book and tape together	$14 for book and tape together

Name: _____

Street Address: _____

City, State, ZIP: _____

Daytime Phone: _____

E-Mail Address (optional): _____

☐ Check Payable to: Dr. Kathryn Vullo   ☐ MasterCard   ☐ Visa

Credit Card Information

Card Number: _____ Expiration Date: _____

Name as it appears on card: _____

Address Associated with card: _____

About The Author

Dr. Kathryn Vullo received her doctorate in Clinical Psychology from the University of Buffalo in 1993, with specialization in health psychology. Her private practice centers around helping people understand how their thoughts and feelings affect their daily choices. By educating people how to recognize their stressors and behavioral patterns and teaching them how to take control over her life, she has helped hundreds of people change their health behaviors, including smoking, diet, and pain management.

Dr. Ronald Vullo received his doctorate in Education from the University of Buffalo in 1992. He is Assistant Professor at Rochester Institute of Technology and is an acknowledged international leader in the fields of educational technology and health care informatics.

Printed in the United States
35831LVS00005B/165